Life as a
PIONEER

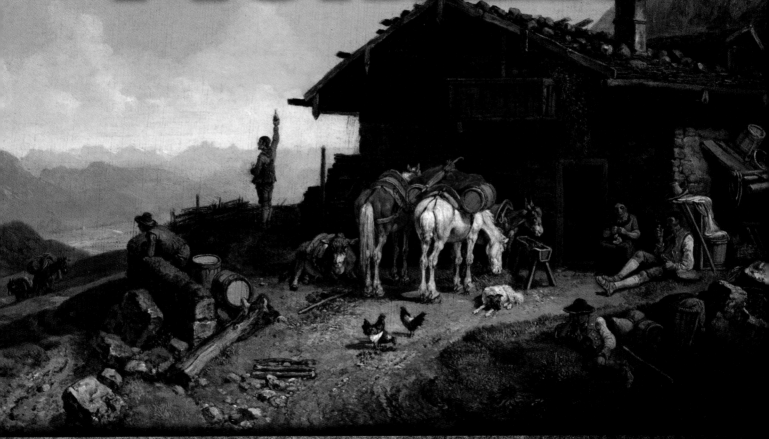

by Kristen Rajczak

Gareth Stevens
Publishing

Please visit our website, www.garethstevens.com. For a free color catalog of all our high-quality books, call toll free 1-800-542-2595 or fax 1-877-542-2596.

Library of Congress Cataloging-in-Publication Data

Rajczak, Kristen.
 Life as a pioneer / Kristen Rajczak.
     p. cm. — (What you didn't know about history)
 Includes bibliographical references and index.
 ISBN 978-1-4339-8420-4 (pbk.)
 ISBN 978-1-4339-8421-1 (6-pack)
 ISBN 978-1-4339-8419-8 (library binding)
 1. Frontier and pioneer life—United States—Juvenile literature 2. United States—Territorial expansion—Juvenile literature. I. Title.
 E179.5.R35 2013
 970.01—dc23

                                        2012018553

First Edition

Published in 2013 by
Gareth Stevens Publishing
111 East 14th Street, Suite 349
New York, NY 10003

Designer: Daniel Hosek and Michael Flynn
Editor: Kristen Rajczak

Photo credits: Cover, pp. 1, 9 SuperStock/Getty Images; p. 5 Howard Pyle/The Bridgeman Art Library/Getty Images; pp. 6, 13 MPI/Getty Images; p. 7 N. Currier/The Bridgeman Art Library/Getty Images; p. 11 courtesy of Library of Congress by Theodore R. Davis; p. 15 Currier and Ives/The Bridgeman Art Library/Getty Images; p. 17 Hulton Archive/Getty Images; p. 19 Ron Embleton/The Bridgeman Art Library/Getty Images; p. 21 Dorling Kindersley/Thinkstock.com.

Printed in the United States of America

CPSIA compliance information: Batch #CW13GS: For further information contact Gareth Stevens, New York, New York at 1-800-542-2595.

CONTENTS

Words in the glossary appear in **bold** type the first time they are used in the text.

MANY PIONEERS

Promises of land and other opportunities drew many people to the American **frontier**. These pioneers settled our country as it grew during the 18th and 19th centuries.

Whether the pioneers' journey took them through the Appalachian Mountains to make their homes in Kentucky or across the Great Plains, the trip was long and hard. However, there was much more to pioneer lives than just heading west! This book will focus mainly on how pioneer families lived once they claimed their land.

Did You Know?

Anyone who makes a discovery or finds a new way of doing something may be called a pioneer. The word comes from an old French word for "foot soldier."

Groups of pioneers often traveled long distances to the places they wanted to settle.

HEADED TO THE FRONTIER

Some of the earliest pioneers were men **exploring** the land or fur trappers. After 1750, big groups made up of families and people from the same area started to travel west on horseback or by wagon.

Journeying with a big group had many advantages. They could carry more supplies and help each other if a wagon wheel broke or a river was hard to cross. Pioneers also thought about safety. A big group meant more people to guard against Native American attacks.

Did You Know?

While the frontier seemed a wild, unsettled place to the pioneers, Native Americans had been living in many areas for hundreds of years. Many pioneers settled on their land illegally.

The big groups traveling west often shaped the close communities pioneers would form on the frontier.

TAKING SHELTER

After their long journey, pioneers started clearing land for farming and finding food and water right away. Sometimes, they lived out of their wagons or tents for weeks after they arrived! Pioneers on the Great Plains sometimes used sod, or mud and grass, to build "soddies." These weren't much more than covered holes in the ground.

The first homes pioneers built were little more than **shacks** that didn't keep out cold, wind, or rain. This led to living conditions that were hard for many to bear.

Did You Know?

Pioneers used newspapers as wallpaper and toilet paper!

Many pioneer families didn't build permanent homes, such as the popular log cabin, until they were sure they were going to stay.

9

WORKING THE LAND

From clearing the land and preparing the soil for planting, to tending and **harvesting** crops, the first few years on the frontier were trying. And the harvest wasn't always as good as farmers hoped.

In addition to the crops grown to sell, pioneers planted gardens in the spring and fall. The fruits and vegetables grown in the "kitchen garden" were an important part of the pioneer **diet**. They dried or jarred much of their garden harvest for use during winter when fresh foods were hard to find.

Did You Know?
In order to eat dried fruit during the winter, pioneers would cook it in water with sugar so it would taste better.

These farmers used a team of oxen, or a kind of male cow, to clear their land.

11

DINNER ON THE FRONTIER

The pioneers ate filling meals to strengthen them for hard work on their land. They hunted animals for meat and roasted them. They ate berries and plants growing near their homes. Though their meals were simple, it took a long time to find and make a pioneer meal.

When supplies were low, pioneer families had to make do with what was on hand. Mashed beans mixed with sweet spices might be eaten in place of pumpkin pie!

Did You Know?

Many pioneers lived too far from the post office or general store to send and receive mail and buy supplies very often. They might only travel "to town" once or twice a year to gather what they needed.

Many pioneer men hunted the meat their families ate.

13

WHAT TO WEAR

How many shirts do you own? If you were a pioneer woman, you would only have two or three dresses in all! Many pioneers couldn't afford brightly colored dyes or cloth other than wool. In fact, in some areas, cloth wasn't available at all. Then, pioneer women had to weave their own.

Since laundry was done by hand, having few clothing choices wasn't always bad. Between gathering enough water, heating it, and making laundry soap, the chore could take all day!

Did You Know?

While breeches—a kind of short pant—were worn by most men during the 18th century, pioneer men wore long pants to keep themselves covered in the fields. Before this, only shepherds and sailors wore long pants!

As more pioneers settled on the frontier, ready-made clothing and cloth became easier to find.

15

WORKING AGE

Pioneer children helped their families from a young age. They brought water in from the well or milked cows and collected eggs if the family owned livestock.

Both girls and boys started working on the family farm at about 10 years old. Girls in other parts of the country didn't work outside the house much during the 1700s and 1800s. However, since pioneer women needed to know how to rope cattle as well as keep house, girls learned to do both.

Did You Know?

Schoolhouses commonly had one room for students of all ages. Some children had no books to learn from. Others only had the family Bible.

Until they were old enough to work in the fields, pioneer children helped around the house by sewing, cooking, and doing laundry.

17

IN SICKNESS AND HEALTH

Depending on where they settled, pioneers faced heat, icy winters, and dust storms—sometimes before they built a sturdy house in which to live! Illness was a constant worry.

Among those who traveled west, doctors were some of the most needed. They rode on horseback many miles between small frontier **homesteads** to help those who were sick or hurt. Because **medicine** wasn't always available or affordable, frontier doctors had to learn how to use plants to treat illnesses, aches, and pains.

Did You Know?
Some pioneer doctors didn't go to school! They learned about healing as **apprentices**.

Many of the illnesses pioneers faced are easily treated today.

19

PIONEER FUN

Life on the American frontier wasn't all work! Though sometimes they lived miles apart, pioneer neighbors formed close communities that visited and celebrated together.

Groups would host spelling bees at the local schoolhouse. Neighbors made cheese together. During the summer, pioneer communities hosted picnics and dances. Music was a big part of these gatherings. Songs we still know today, such as "Home on the Range" and "Skip to My Lou," were popular for the pioneers to sing and dance to!

Did You Know?

Pioneer children played a game like tag, but they called it fox and geese.

TALL TALES

The pioneers told many stories to pass the time. These "tall tales" also helped draw more people out West. Here are some of the best-known American folk stories from that time.

- **Johnny Appleseed** was said to have scattered apple seeds all over the United States. His story was based on the life of John Chapman, who did plant apple trees throughout the Midwest.

- Stories of folk hero **Pecos Bill** say coyotes raised him! He was a tough rancher who rode a mountain lion and used a rattlesnake as a lasso.

- **Davy Crockett** was a real frontiersman from Tennessee. He claimed to have killed many bears and snakes as a child. These stories grew into tall tales by the time he became a congressman in the 1820s and 1830s!

Davy Crockett

apprentice: someone who learns a trade by working with a skilled person of that trade

diet: the food and drink a person eats

explore: to search in order to find out new things

frontier: the edge of a settled part of a country

harvest: to bring in a crop. Also, the crop itself.

homestead: the home and land received from the US government

medicine: a drug taken to make a sick person well

permanent: meant to last a long time

shack: a small, roughly built shelter

FOR MORE INFORMATION

Books

Benoit, Peter. *The Louisiana Purchase*. New York, NY: Children's Press, 2012.

Sanford, William R. *Daniel Boone: Courageous Frontiersman*. Berkeley Heights, NJ: Enslow Publishers, 2012.

Websites

Games and Activities of Pioneer Children
www.ndstudies.org/resources/activites/es/pioneer.html
Learn how to play some of the games pioneer children enjoyed.

Tall Tales
www.kidscomputerlab.org/index.php/language-arts/tall-tales-activity/
Read some famous American tall tales. Then, write one of your own.

$\mathcal{I}$NDEX